Start TO Finish
Second Series

FROM
Strawberry TO Jam

• LISA OWINGS

 LERNER PUBLICATIONS COMPANY • Minneapolis

Lerner Publications Company
A division of Lerner Publishing Group, Inc.
241 First Avenue North
Minneapolis, MN 55401 USA

For reading levels and more information, look up this title at www.lernerbooks.com.

Library of Congress Cataloging-in-Publication Data

Owings, Lisa, author.
    From strawberry to jam / by Lisa Owings.
        pages   cm. — (Start to finish. Second series)
    Includes index.
    ISBN 978–1–4677–6022–5 (lib. bdg. : alk. paper)
    ISBN 978–1–4677–6289–2 (eBook)
    1. Canning and preserving—Juvenile literature.
    2. Jam—Juvenile literature. 3. Canned strawberries—Juvenile literature. I. Title.
TP371.3.O95 2015
664'.80475—dc23   2014025229

Manufactured in the United States of America
1 – CG – 12/31/14

TABLE OF Contents

First, jam makers pick ripe strawberries.	4
Then they wash the berries.	6
Next, jam makers cut up the berries.	8
They mix the berries with sugar.	10
Then they cook the mixture.	12
Next, jam makers pour the jam into jars.	14
Then they put the jars in boiling water.	16
Next, they let the jam cool.	18
Finally, the jam is ready to eat!	20
Glossary	22
Further Information	23
Index	24

I love strawberry jam on toast! How is it made?

First, jam makers pick ripe strawberries.

Jam can be made from all kinds of fruits. Strawberries are one of the most common fruits for jam. Jam makers pick ripe strawberries in the spring and the summer. They need several cups of strawberries to make jam.

Then they wash the berries.

Jam makers wash the strawberries well.
Then they cut off the stems and the leaves.

Next, jam makers cut up the berries.

Some jam makers cut the strawberries into small pieces. Others **crush** the berries. This helps the strawberries release their sugars and juices.

They mix the berries with sugar.

Jam makers place the berries in a large pot. Then they add sugar. Often they add **acidic** lemon juice or **pectin** to help thicken the mixture. The jam makers stir everything together.

Then they cook the mixture.

Jam makers bring the pot to a boil. They cook the jam
for several minutes until it begins to thicken. They test the
thickness by letting a spoonful of jam cool. The spoonful
shows what the **consistency** of the finished jam will be.

Next, jam makers pour the jam into jars.

When the jam is thick enough, they pour it into jars.
The jars must be clean first. Jam makers put lids on
the jars and make sure to seal them tightly.

Then they put the jars in boiling water.

The jam makers put the jam jars in a large pot of boiling water. They use a special tool called a **jar lifter**. The jars boil for about ten minutes. This makes the jam safe to eat and keeps it from **spoiling**.

Next, they let the jam cool.

The jam makers use their jar lifters to take out the jars. They set them out for a day or so to cool. As the jars cool, the jam gets firmer.

Finally, the jam is ready to eat!

After cooling, the jam can be spread on many delicious things. Extra jam can usually be stored in the jars for up to one year. That means you can have a taste of summer in the middle of winter. Just open a fresh jar of jam!

Glossary

acidic: having a sour taste. Acid is one of the ingredients that helps jam thicken.

consistency: the firmness or thickness of a substance, such as a liquid

crush: to press or squeeze something so that it loses its shape

jar lifter: a tool that allows a person to lift and move hot jars without touching them. Jar lifters keep jam makers from burning themselves.

pectin: a substance in some fruits that helps jam thicken. Jam makers can use fruits with a lot of pectin in them or buy pectin from a store.

spoiling: becoming rotten or unsafe to eat

Further Information

Borgert-Spaniol, Megan. *Fruit Group*. Minneapolis: Bellwether Media, 2012. Find out why eating fruits is so important.

Fruit and Veggie Color Champions
http://www.foodchamps.org
Learn about fruits and vegetables through fun games and activities on this website.

How Food Is Preserved
http://sciencewithkids.com/Science-Articles/How-food-is-preserved.html
Learn how people have preserved their food since ancient times.

Nelson, Robin. *Strawberries*. Minneapolis: Lerner Publications, 2009. Check out this book to learn about the life cycle of strawberries.

Preserving the School Garden Harvest
http://www.kidsgardening.org/node/12020
Making jam is just one way of preserving food. Ask a parent or a teacher to help you learn about other methods at home or at school.

Index

boil, 12, 16

cook, 12
cool, 18
crush, 8

mix, 10

pick, 4
pour, 14

wash, 6

Photo Acknowledgments

The images in this book are used with the permission of:
© Volosina/iStock/Thinkstock, p. 1; © Andy Crawford/
Thinkstock, p. 3; © Mijang Ka/Moment/Getty Images, p. 5;
© iStockphoto.com/goldyrocks, p. 7; © Profimedia.CZ a.s./
Alamy, p. 9; © Simon Watson/Photolibrary/Getty Images,
p. 11; © RF Food Shots/Alamy, p. 13; © moriyu/Moment/
Getty Images, p. 15; © Zuma Press, Inc./Alamy, p. 17;
© Lucy Lambriex/Moment Open/Getty Images, p. 19;
© Vstock LLC/Getty Images, p. 21.

Front cover © ddsign_stock/istock/Thinkstock.

Main body text set in Arta Std Book 20/26.
Typeface provided by International Typeface Corp.